YOUR WORDS
YOUR VOICE

Cover Page
Artist: Lorelei McDaniel Broxson
Inspired by Poem: "The Angel Who Lost His Wings"

https://facebook.com/Lorelei.Broxson.Art
loreleilynn@hotmail.com

Your Words
Your Voice
An Invitation to Expression

Bahareh Amidi

Poets who are Travel Companions in Your Words Your Voice

© The Journey by Mary Oliver. The Atlantic Monthly Press. (May 1986)

© If You Praise a Word, It Turns Into a Poem. Copyright held by Caitlin Weber.

© When Someone Deeply Listens to You. Finding What You Didn't Lose: Expressing Your Truth and Creativity Through Poem-Making. Permission granted by the author.

© A Voice Through the Door. Rumi: Voice of Longing by Coleman Barks. Sound True Publications (2002)

ISBN 978-9948-18-438-6

The Angel Who Lost His Wings

Once upon a time there was an Angel

An Angel who lost his wings

He was walking through life wondering what fault

had made his wings disappear

He saw the birds flying in the sky and the bees buzzing around

He saw a rock by the river and he sat

and sat

and sat

after years of sitting he decided to walk again

and look for his wings

That is when he started to fly

wingless with heart

Your Words Your Voice

This is where we begin this journey… knowing that each and every one of us has wings and each and every one of us can fly.

Today this flight takes the form of writing about feelings and images.

All you need is a blank piece of paper, a pen, and an open heart.

If I were to tell you in a capsule what poetry therapy is…

I would take a blank piece of paper and say…

Each and every blank piece of paper you see anywhere in the world is an invitation to your heart and soul…

Get a blank piece of paper and place it in front of you, and put both your hands on your heart. Then, as if in a pouring motion, allow what is in your heart to pour out onto the paper.

The important thing to remember is that there are no rights or wrongs. Nothing has to rhyme or make sense; it just has to flow from the heart.

There is only one rule: do not block yourself, just let yourself go with the flow. Trust yourself and your inner voice.

You might say to yourself now, "But I do not write poetry," or, "I am not a good writer." No problem at all!

All you have to do is to let your heart flow and write.

Go back to the poem on the previous page, read it one more time, and then repeat any sentences, phrases, or words that touched you.

Then, please say them out loud.

The purpose of saying them aloud is that words take on a new life when we give them a voice.

This is also called "mirroring" the lines to the poet, the person who has written this poem… which in this case happens to be me... so the person feels heard.

If I were sitting next to you, I would hear the words in your voice and this might give the words a new meaning to me.

Now just allow yourself this space, the gift of this moment.

I will suggest a couple of prompts to put on your blank page, but you can start anywhere you like.

It can be a phrase from this poem, or it can come from any-where, as long as it is from your heart, or your gut, or the place of your inner truth.

When you start writing, just write images and feelings that come to you at this time. There is no right or wrong.

You will find three prompts on the following page to get you started. Just finish any of these sentences or start with some-thing else, anything. Now free write for about 3 to 5 minutes.

It doesn't have to be in any particular form or style of poetry.

Let your wings find flight and write. Imagine I am sitting next to you and I am writing as well. I always write when you write.

Once upon a time there was...

Or

Once upon a time there was not...

Or

Walking through life wondering...

The following blank page is an invitation ....

Now that you have written, if there is someone close by, ask him or her if you can read it to them.

If not, imagine you are reading what you wrote to me, and please know that I am listening. The essence of this is to give your words a voice.

Now, just consider how it felt for you to write this… and how did it feel to read it out loud? If you have read it out loud to someone ask him or her to mirror back a few words or lines to you without judgment or analysis.

How does it feel for you to hear your own words in another's voice?

Did you say anything in your writing that surprised you?

Sometimes our own words teach us if we let them.

The beauty of poetry therapy is that it is available for you at any time, anywhere.

All you need to do is simply read a poem, any poem from any source, or recite one from memory, then write a few lines on the paper and let your words find flight and flow.

Whether it is English or your mother tongue, use whatever language makes you feel more at home. Our voice has no boundaries and extends over borders and walls.

There are millions of poems to choose from, but here I will just provide a few sample poems to help you begin on your path. As before, read the poem, sit with it for a while, say sentences, phrases or words that touched you out loud and then consider a prompt suggested or choose your own.

If You Praise a Word, It Turns Into a Poem

Praise to this poem

    for letting me write it.

To book titles

    that give away clues.

Praise to the time on a watch

    so I am not late.

To the shell

    that washes upon the shore for me.

Praise to the fly's eye

    with which he sees everything.

To the grass

    that whistles when I blow it.

Praise to the mud

    that makes me dirty when I play.

To the thunder

    that warns me of a lightning flash.

Praise to my name

    without which I'd be no one.

To this poem

    for letting me write it.

Caitlin Weber, 4th grade

Just as Caitlin has written of a poem, book, watch, shell, fly, etc.. make a list of simple things in your life and make them a part of your own poem.

Consider starting with:

Praise to....

Or

No praise to.....

Or anything that works for you

The following blank page is an invitation ....

Here is another poem. This one is from John Fox – my teacher
of Poetry Therapy

WHEN SOMEONE DEEPLY LISTENS TO YOU

When someone deeply listens to you

it is like holding out a dented cup

you've had since childhood

and watching it fill up with

cold, fresh water.

When it balances on top of the brim,

you are understood.

When it overflows and touches your skin,

you are loved.

When someone deeply listens to you,

the room where you stay

starts a new life

and the place where you wrote

your first poem

begins to glow in your mind's eye.

It is as if gold has been discovered!

When someone deeply listens to you,

your bare feet are on the earth

and a beloved land that seemed distant

is now at home within you.

— John Fox

You can start writing anywhere, so this is just an idea, just let your heart flow and your words pour out of you.

Now consider starting to write from:

When someone deeply listens to me...

Or
When someone does not deeply listen to me....

Or
when I do not listen to you..

Or
When I do not listen to myself...

Or
Holding out a dented cup...

Or any line that works as a start for you.

The following blank page is an invitation ....

Here is another poem. This one is from Rumi, a master of writing freely:

A Voice Through The Door

Sometimes you hear a voice through the door
calling you, as fish out of water
hear the waves, or a hunting falcon
hears the drum's Come back. Come back.

This turning toward what you deeply love
saves you. Read the book of your life,
which has been given you.

A voice comes to your soul saying,
Lift your foot. Cross over.

Move into emptiness
of question and answer and question.

— Rumi

Consider writing from:

Sometimes I hear a voice…

Or

Sometimes I do not hear a voice…

Or

When I read the book of my life…

Or any start you choose…

The following blank page is an invitation ....

And another poem called 'The Journey'…

THE JOURNEY

One day you finally knew
what you had to do, and began,
though the voices around you
kept shouting
their advice—
though the whole house
began to tremble
and you felt the old tug
at your ankles.
"Mend my life!"
each voice cried.
But you didn't stop.
You knew what you had to do,
though the wind pried
with its stiff fingers
at the very foundations—
though their melancholy
was terrible.

It was already late
enough, and a wild night,
and the road full of fallen
branches and stones.
But little by little,
as you left their voices behind
the stars began to burn
through the sheets of clouds,
and there was a new voice,
which you slowly recognized as your
own,
that kept you company
as you strode deeper and deeper
into the world,
determined to do
the only thing you could do—
determined to save
the only life you could save.

— Mary Oliver

Once you have read it, consider writing starting with

One day I finally knew...

Or

One day I did not yet know...

Or

The only thing I could do....

Or

Little by little...

Or

There was a new voice...

The following blank page is an invitation ....

At any time, know that you can come to a blank piece of paper and write. You will find answers or maybe you will find questions.

The beauty of writing in this way is that as you start to do it regularly, you become somehow more connected to yourself and to the universe around you. You may also find that solitude calls you, if that is what you need in your life.

The most important part to remember is this:

When you see a blank piece of paper, it is an invitation… to your heart and soul.

Be open… write… and let your words find flight with your voice.

Enjoy,

Always
InLight

To learn more about Poetry Therapy and Healing:

- The Institute for Poetic Medicine
- National Association for Poetry Therapy
- The Creative "Righting" Center

For additional poems:
- Poetry Daily
- Poetry Foundation

Your workshop was so powerful and life changing for me
Artist, Colorado

Abu Dhabi
TED

You opened the door of writing poetry into my life
Spiritual Companion

Your Words

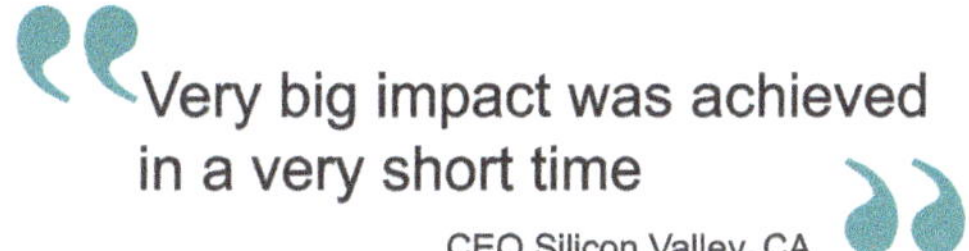

CEO Silicon Valley, CA

Board Member Chemical Company Mexico City

Your Voice

To experience YOUR WORDS YOUR VOICE live
visit BahareLIVE on YOUTUBE